Triniti's First Steps with Jesus

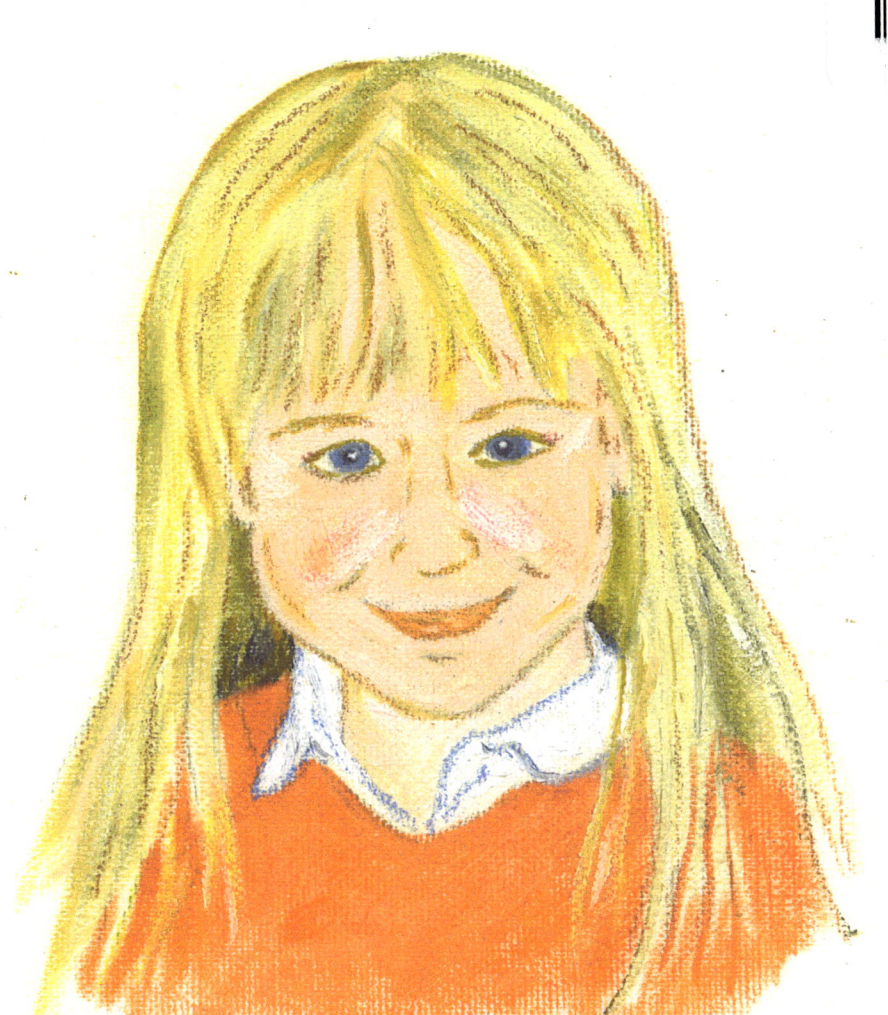

Written and Illustrated by Barbara Haney

AuthorHouse™
1663 Liberty Drive, Suite 200
Bloomington, IN 47403
www.authorhouse.com
Phone: 1-800-839-8640

First published by AuthorHouse 3/4/2009

ISBN: 978-1-4389-3453-2 (sc)

Printed in the United States of America
Bloomington, Indiana

This book is printed on acid-free paper.

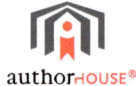

author HOUSE®

This book is dedicated to

My five children

Owen, Bonnie, Nancy, Mark and Kristan

All my grandchildren

And all my great grandchildren

This book contains bible truths. It is for you whether you are five or ninety-five. These are words and ways to live to obtain God's blessings for you and your loved ones. You are never too young or too old to begin to speak and live the way God intends.

Acknowledgements

My heartfelt thanks to each of the following:

The Holy Spirit for suggesting I write this book.

My friend, Nancy Kerr for agreeing with Him and for editing all my rough drafts.

My daughter, Nancy Enneking for the hours spent scanning and printing all my art work.

Thank you to the following for bible teachings:

Kenneth and Gloria Copeland

Keith Moore

Creflo A Dollar

Douglas Graves

Andrew Wommack

Andrew Fox

Holy Bible NIV [New International Version]

And many others too numerous to mention.

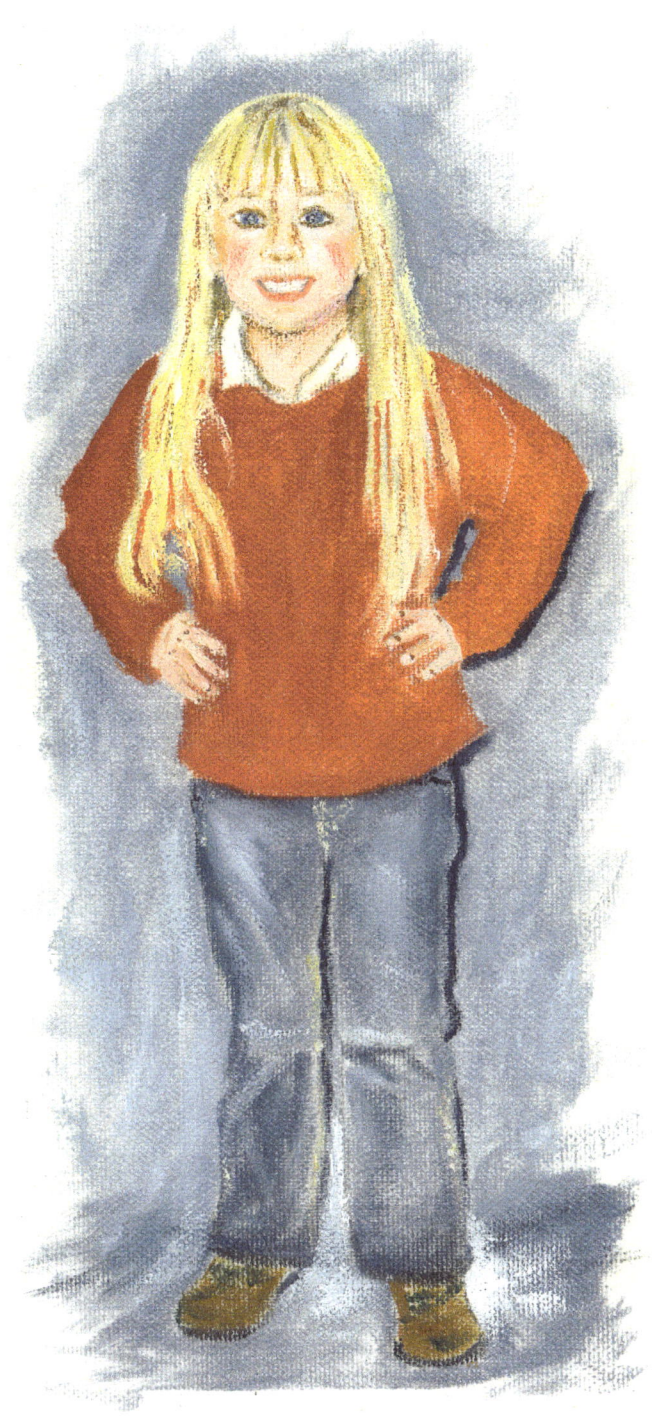

My name is Triniti. I'm just a kid. I want to tell you about my Jesus.

My name is just like God. Trinity means Father, Son and Holy Spirit. My Jesus is the "Son".

I love Jesus and He loves me.[1] He loves you, too. Jesus helps me to be good. He tells me to be kind[2] to every one. He says I should love my neighbors.[3] And I do.

1. 1 John 4:19   We love because he first loved us.
2. 1 Thess 5:15   ...but always try to be kind each other.
3. Gal 5:14   ...love your neighbor as yourself.

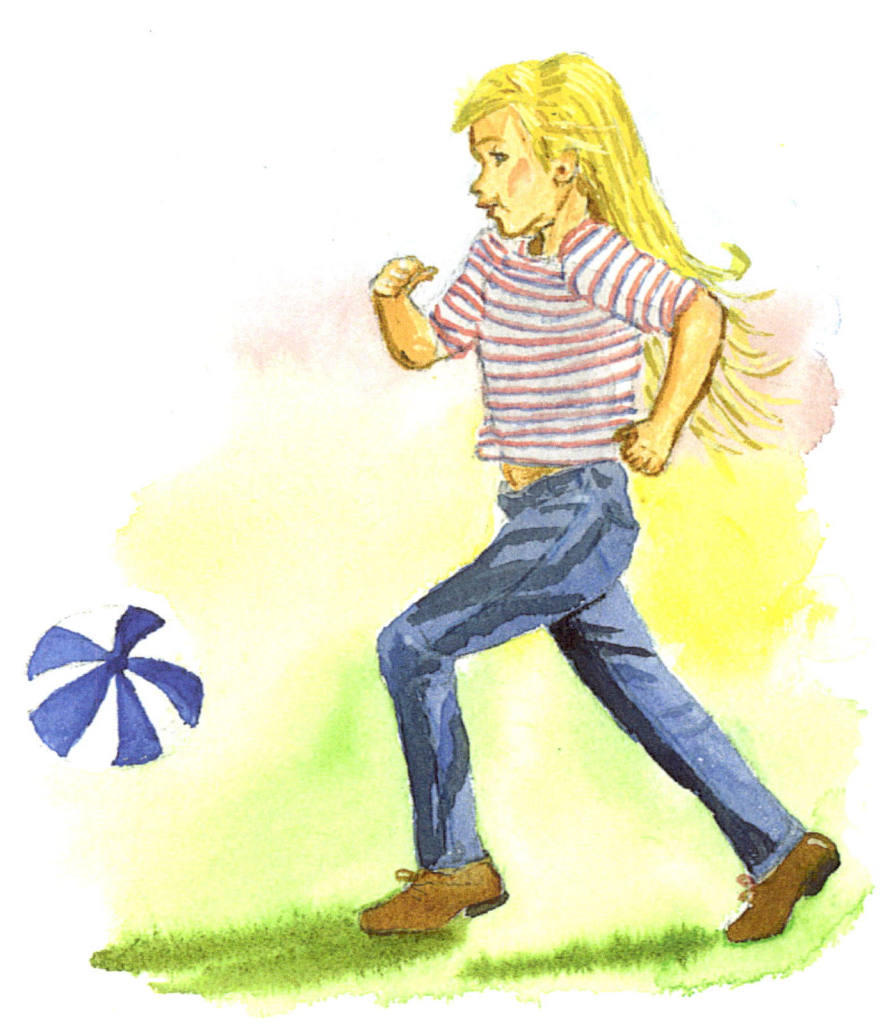

Protection

One day at Sunday School I asked Jesus to come into my heart. When I did, His Holy Spirit came to live in me.[1] Sometimes the Holy Spirit talks to me out loud, it seems to me. But Nan says He is really speaking in my heart. Nan says the Holy Spirit is my protector[2] if I will listen to hear His voice and obey. One day my ball rolled out into the street. I started to run after it, but the Holy Spirit said, "Stay on the sidewalk." My Daddy went out in the street and got my ball for me. He said streets are for cars, not little girls.

1. John 14:16-17 And I will ask the Father, and he will give you another Counselor to be with you forever the Spirit of Truth. The world cannot accept him, because it neither sees him nor knows him. But you know him, for he lives with you and will be in you.

2. Psalms 91:14 "Because he loves me," says the Lord, "I will rescue him, I will protect him, for he acknowledges my name. He will call upon me, and I will answer him; I will be with him in trouble, I will deliver him and honor him."

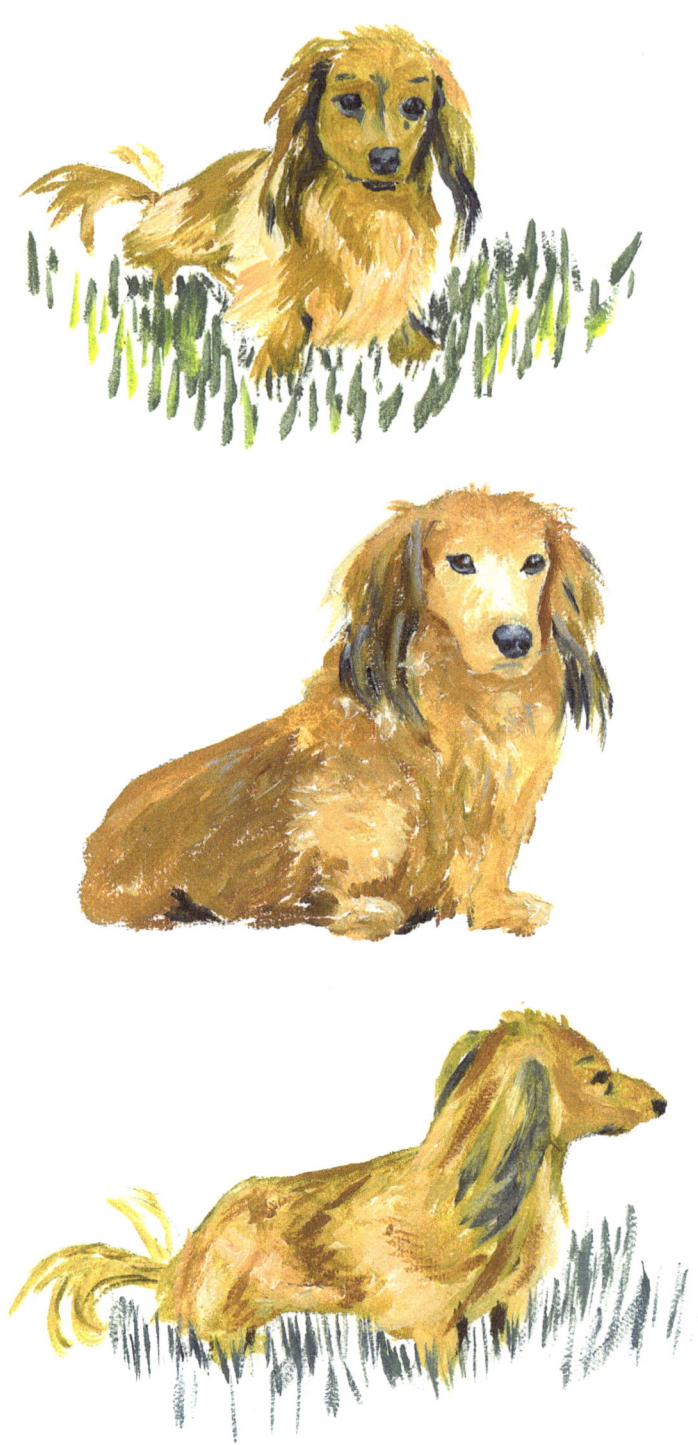

Life Plan

Jesus walks with me in my Nan's garden. Nan is my grandmother. She has so many beautiful flowers. Squirrels and quail come to visit her. Nan has three dogs. When they see the squirrels they come a barking. Daisy is the name of one of the dogs and the squirrels drive her nuts! I think they like to tease her. I love my Nan. She is very patient and kind and always makes me feel loved.[1] Jesus says that love is the greatest gift. My Nan says that Jesus has a plan for my life. He has a plan for your life, too. It is up to us to find out what that plan is. We must keep asking Him in our prayers to show us this plan. Jesus says we can do all things because He makes us strong.[2]

1. I Cor 13:4 Love is patient, love is kind.

2. I Cor 1:8 He will keep you strong to the end.; Eph 6:10 Finally, be strong in the Lord

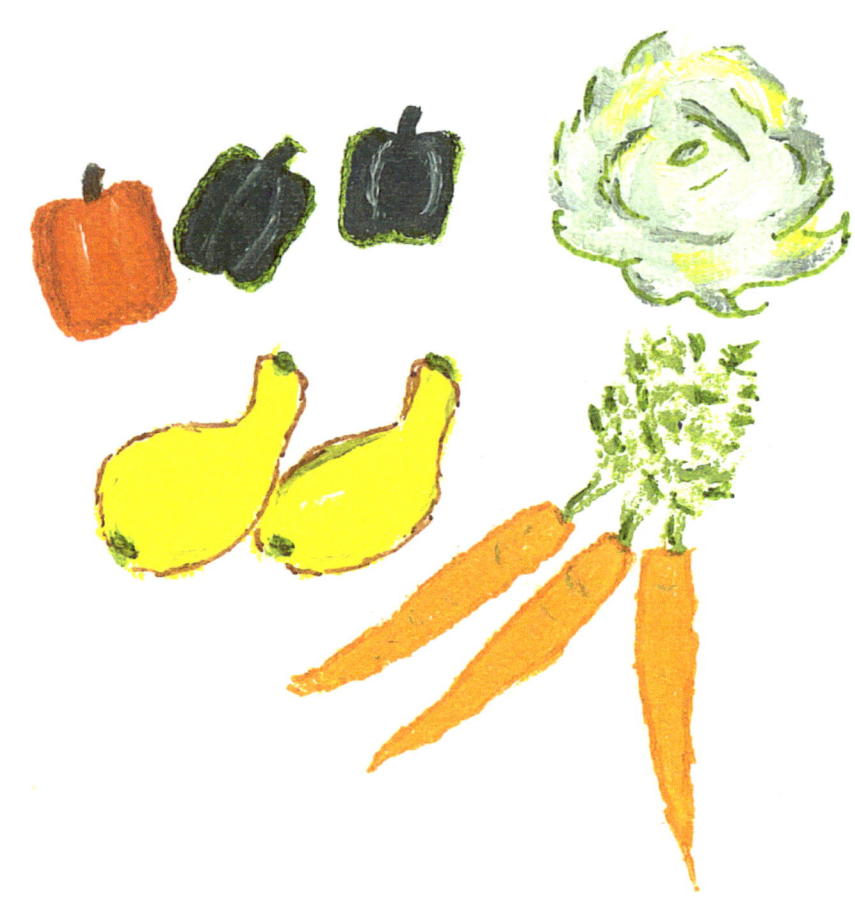

Seed, Time And Harvest

My great grandmother MeeMa and my Nan planted a garden. Little plants are coming up. It will take a month or more, and then vegetables will start to grow. MeeMa says that is how we are to live in this world. God's plan is for us to plant seed, wait a time, then comes fruit and we can pick it. She said that she tithes[1] to God and gives offerings to her church. Then God gives back to her. Tithes and offerings are money.   So I give part of my allowance at Sunday school for God. This is the "seed" that I am planting. MeeMa said that many years ago my Nan and Papa were so excited. They phoned to tell her that they had started tithing to their church and were surprised to discover that the rest of their money went farther than ever before.

1. Luke 6:38 Give and it shall be given to you, good measure, pressed down shaken together shall men give unto your bosom.; Mal 3:8   How do we rob God? In tithes and offerings.; Mal 3:10 Bring the whole tithe into the store house.

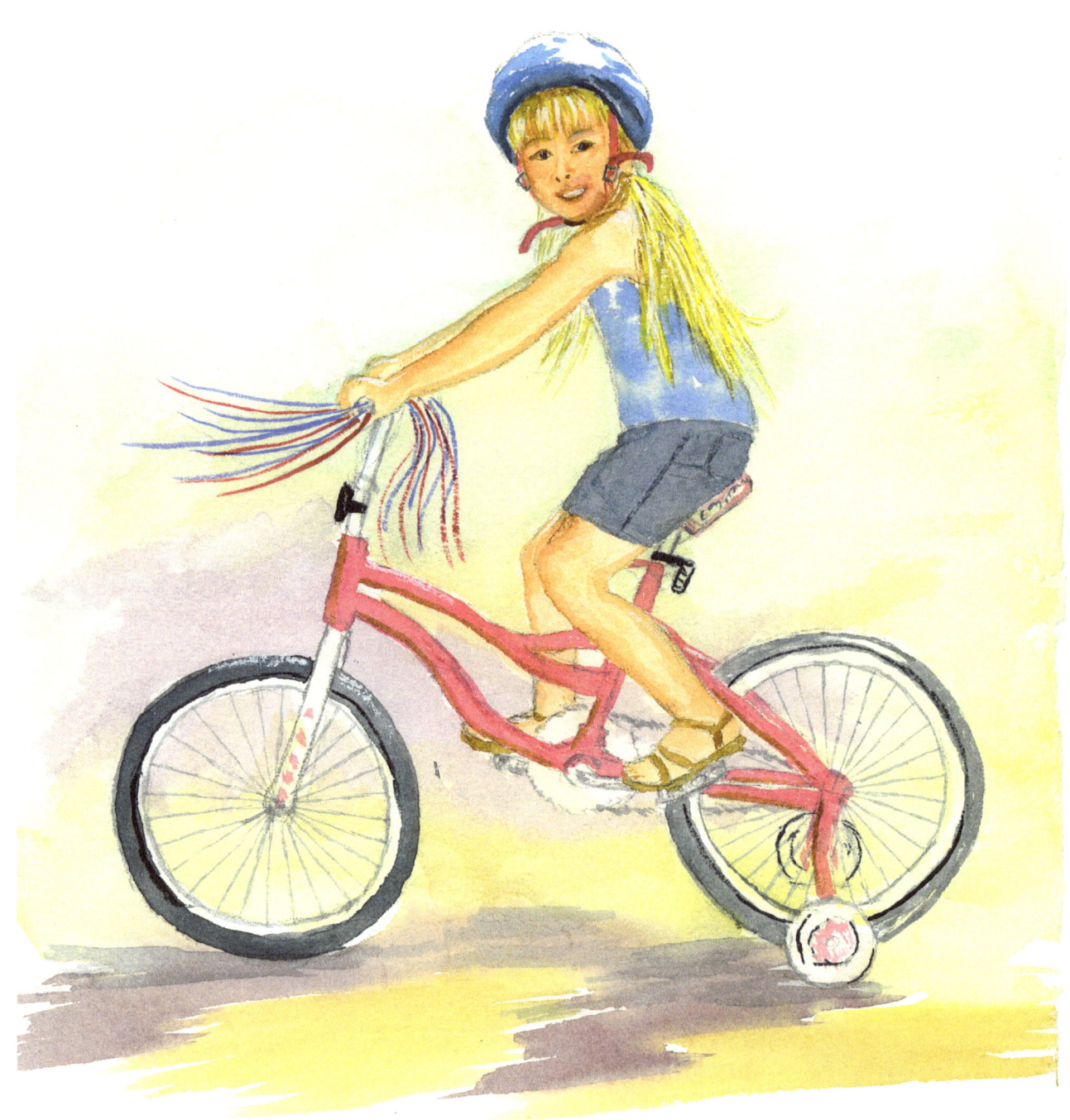

Prosperity And Healing

Nan and MeeMa took me shopping for a bicycle. We found one just the right size for me. We also got a helmet to protect my head if I fall. I got to ride my bike through the store to the checkout stand. When we got home, MeeMa and Nan oiled the chain and tightened the bolts. Then Nan ran beside me as I rode my new bike. Oh, oh, I turned too sharp and fell over. My knee was skinned and I cried and cried. Nan cleaned my knee and put some medicine on it and she said, "I speak to you skinned knee. Be healed." Then she told me that by Jesus' wounds I was healed.[1]

I love my Nan and I love my Jesus. You can speak to your hurts, too.

1. Isaiah 53:5   But he was pierced for our transgressions, he was crushed for our iniquities; the punishment that brought us peace was upon him, and by his wounds we are healed.

2. Mark 16:18   They will place their hands on sick people and they will get well

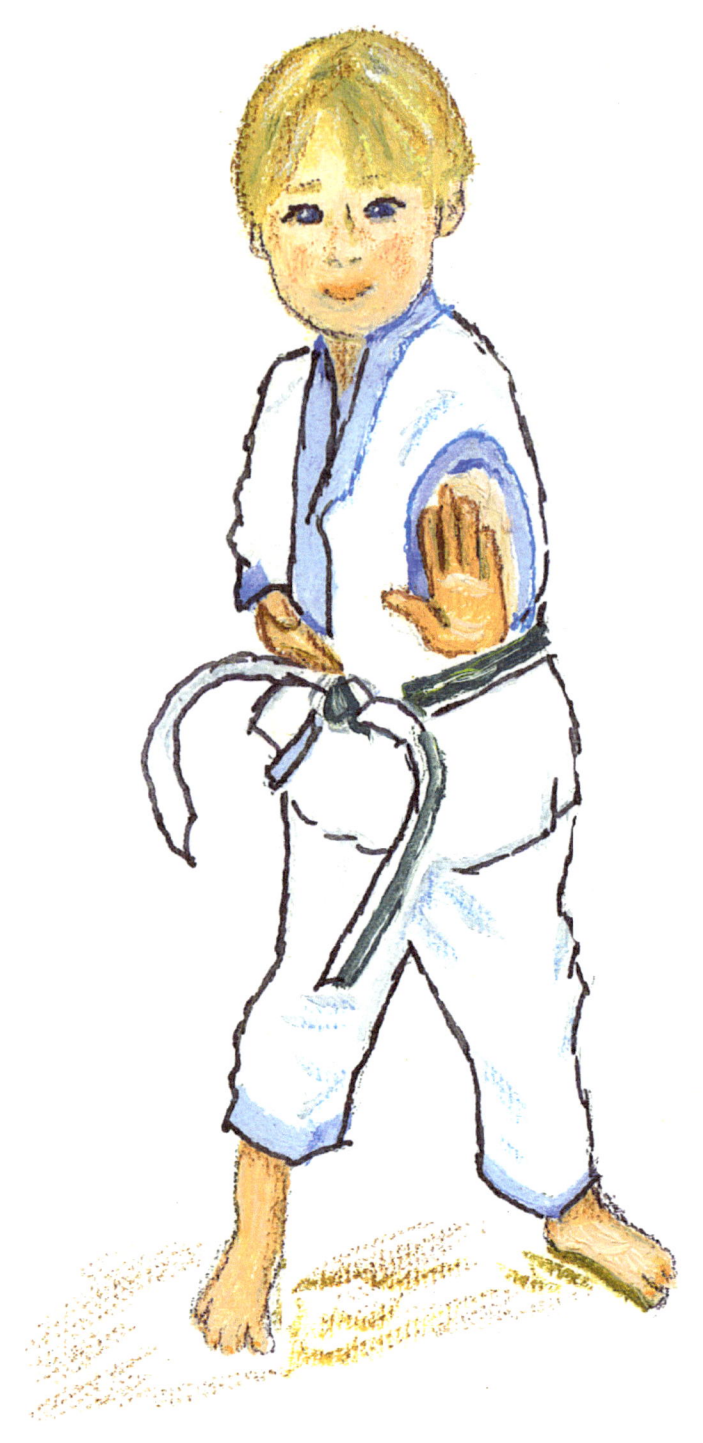

Jesus My Protector

Sometimes at night when I am in bed I become frightened and think something is in my room. Nan said when that happens I am to say, "In Jesus name, get out of my room!"[1] Then everything feels good again and I can go to sleep. Nan says that when I do this, I am speaking to the mountain (anything that is a problem or an illness).[2] Jesus said if I ask anything in His name He would do it for me. That means He will shoo away anything that is scaring me. Jesus is our healer and our protector.

1. James 4:7   Resist the devil and he will flee from you.

2. Mark 11:23-24   Have faith in God. Jesus answered. "I tell you the truth, if anyone says to the mountain, go throw yourself into the sea, and does not doubt in his heart but believes that what he says will happen, it will be done for him.; John 14:14   Jesus said - You may ask me for anything in my name and I will do it.

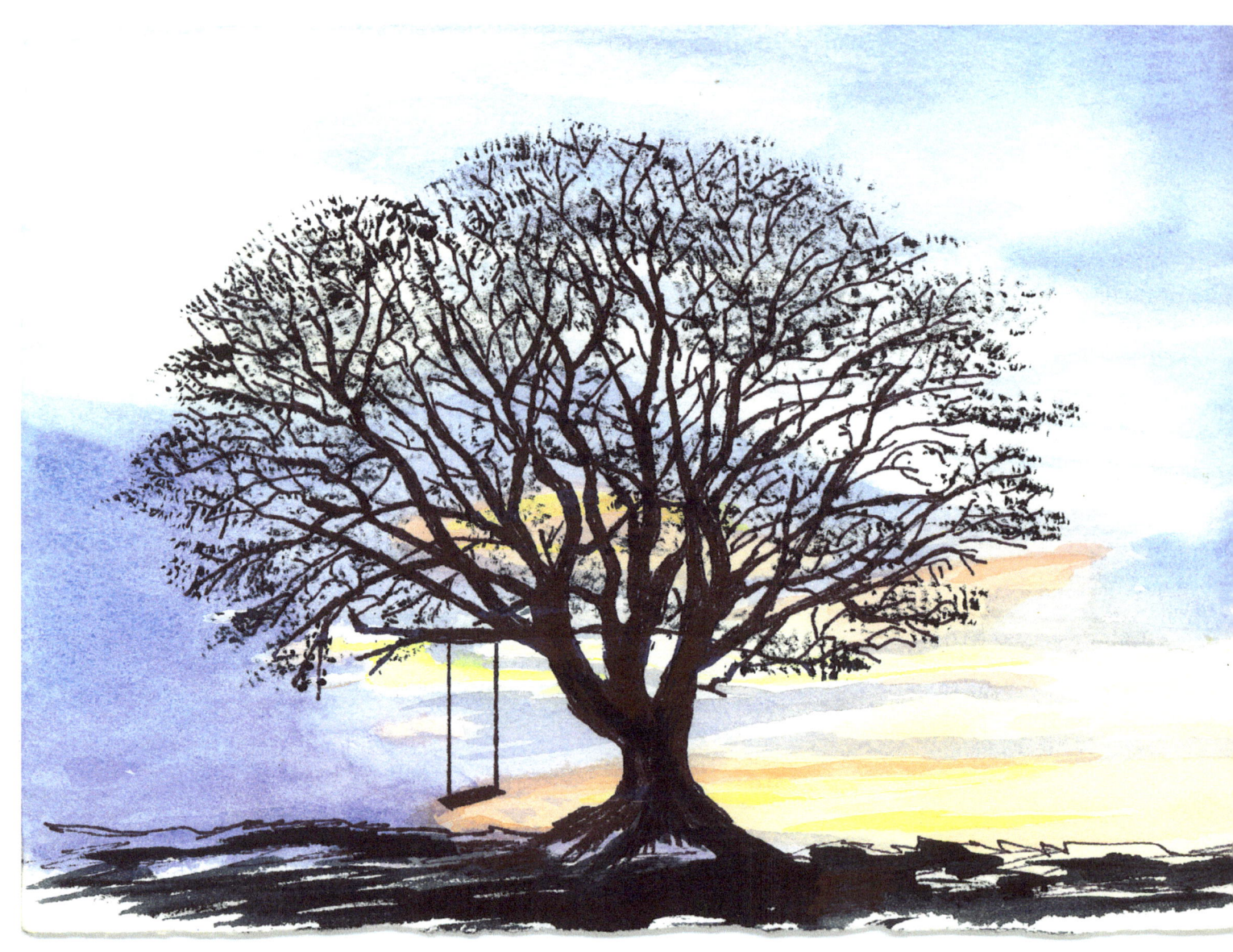

Listening To The Spirit

One day Nan was talking about an accident that happened. Her friend who was telling her about it asked, "How could a loving God allow that to happen to that Christian family?" MeeMa said, "That was not the right question." She said the right question is, "Why didn't someone in that Christian family hear and obey the Holy Spirit when He told them, 'Do not go that way,' or 'Wait ten minutes before leaving'."

We must listen to hear His instructions.[1]

Proverbs 4:13   Hold on to instructions, do not let it go: guard it well for it is your life.

Proverbs 13:13   He who scorns instructions will pay for it.

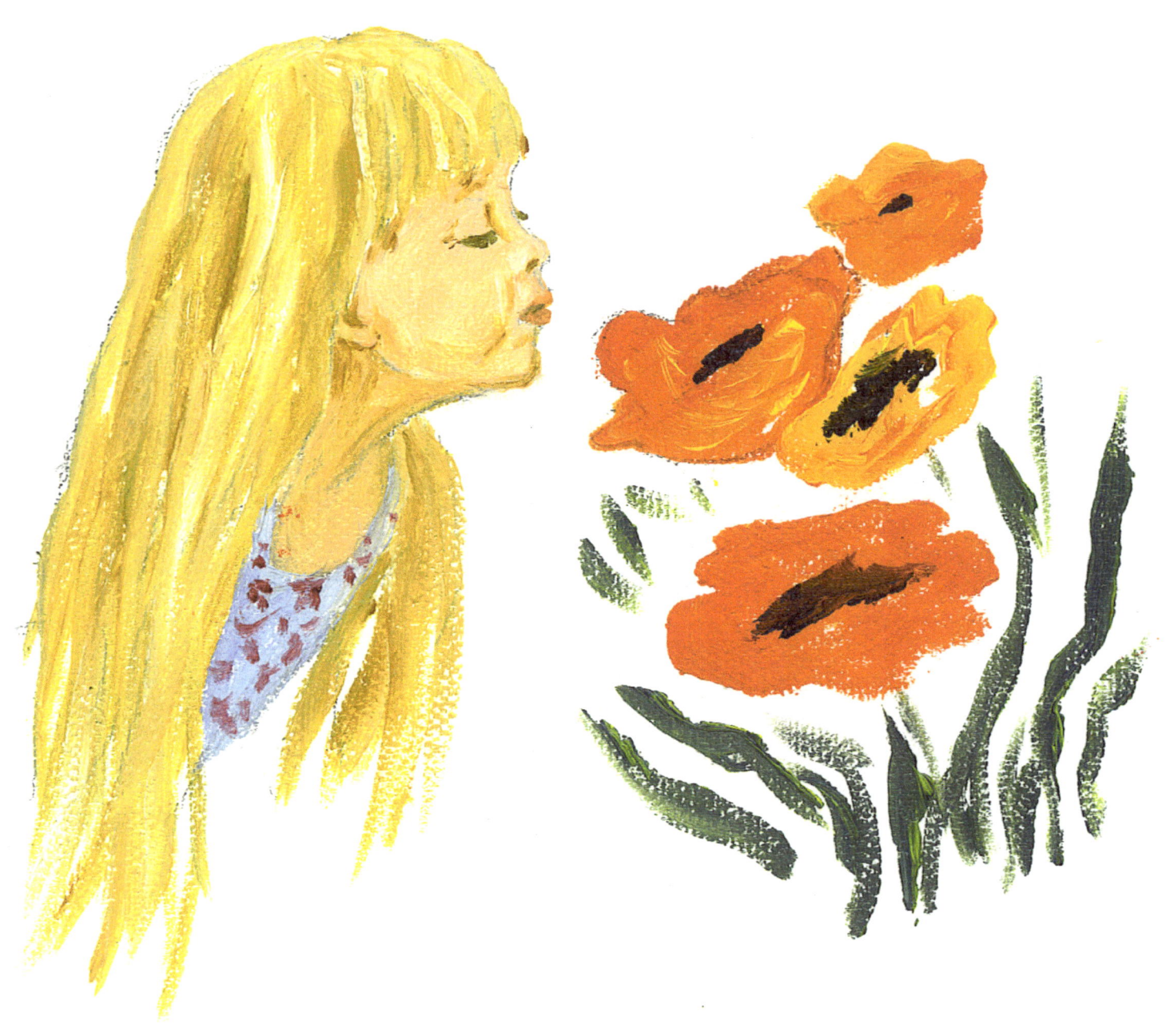

Speaking The Word

MeeMa says we should start speaking the word of God now so that our lives will be better. God calls things that are not as though they were.[1] That means when I am sick with a cold, I must not say: "I'm sick." Rather I should say: "By His stripes I am healed." Then I should speak to the cold and say, "Cold, I speak to you in the name of Jesus: Be gone! I speak to you pain in my throat: Pain be gone! In Jesus name."[2] And you know what? It works every time.

I am so blessed! And you will be, too, if you have faith and do these things that Jesus taught us.

1. Romans 4:17 The God who gives hope to the dead and calls things that are not as though they were.

2. Isaiah 53:5 And by his wounds we are healed.

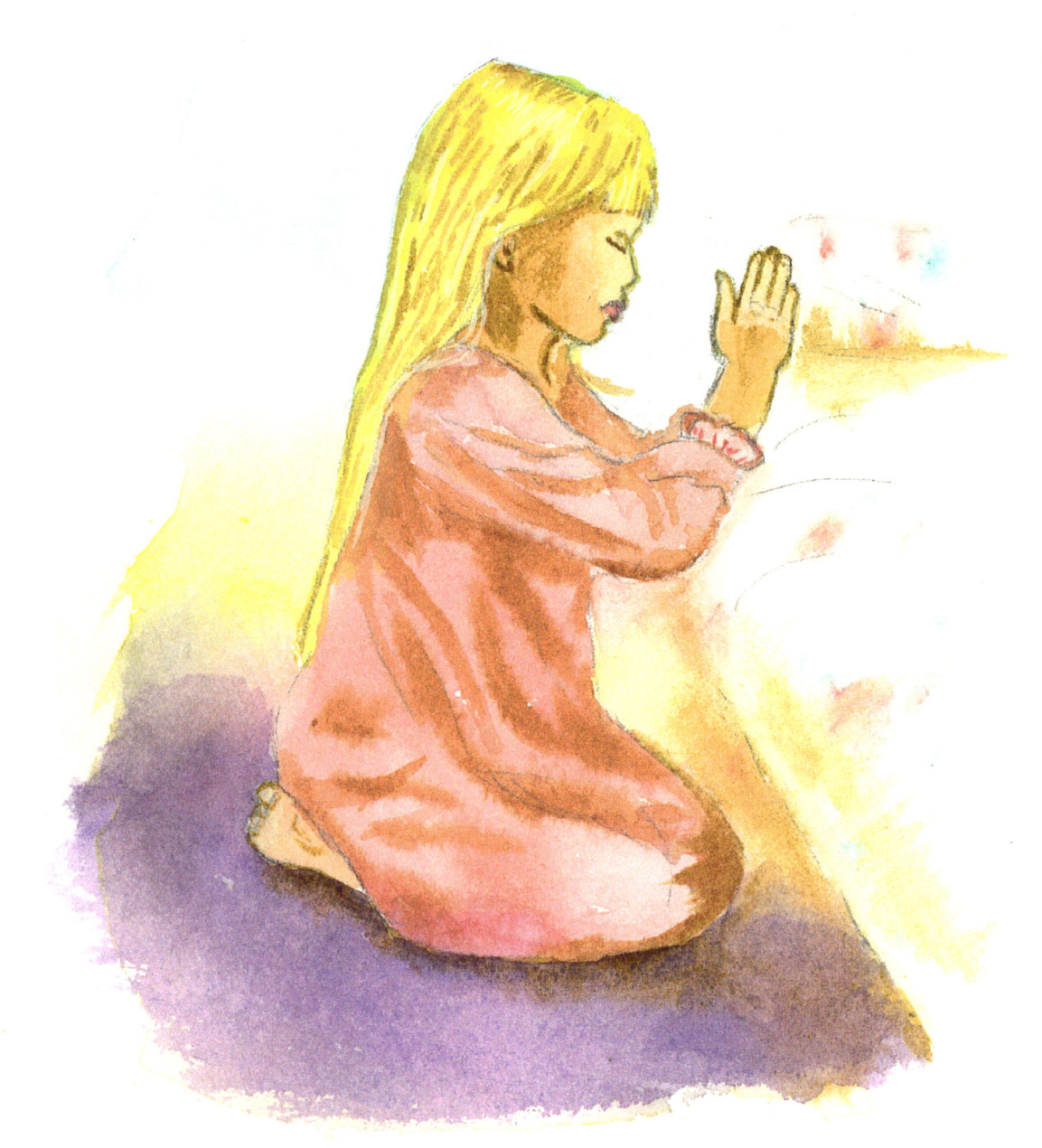

Triniti's Prayer

Dear Reader,

I pray that you will start right now to live your life like Jesus wants you to live. You will be glad that you did. Always remember that Jesus is Lord and He wants to bless you. Please invite Him into your heart right now. My Jesus wants to be your Jesus, too.

Love,

Triniti

Nan's Prayer

Dear Reader,

Think about someone in your life that you know loves you very much. That person wants to spend time with you and talk to you and do special things for you. When someone loves you they want the very best for your life.

God is like that, but because He is God, He can love you so much more than any human ever could. He wants to spend time with you. He wants to talk to you, so He gave you the bible to read that tells of his love and promises for your life. He wants to do special things for you. He sent His baby boy, Jesus, down here to earth to grow up and show you how to live a blessed life. He gave you the Holy Spirit to guide you into that blessed life.

I pray that you will always remember that God loves you.

Nan [Nancy Enneking]

[I am Triniti's grandmother]

A Special Message To Families

Dear Reader,

It is a blessing and obligation to teach your children about God's plan for their life. Let them know that God gave them a special gift. They will be happiest when they recognize their special talent from God and start using it. Tell them, "Whatever God has called you to be - be the very best you can be!!"

I love you, Jesus loves you and Jesus is Lord.

MeeMa   [Barbara Haney]

[I am Triniti's great grandmother]

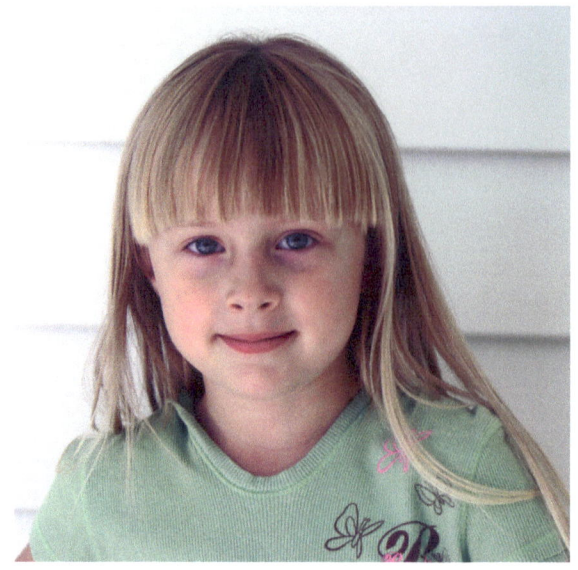

niti

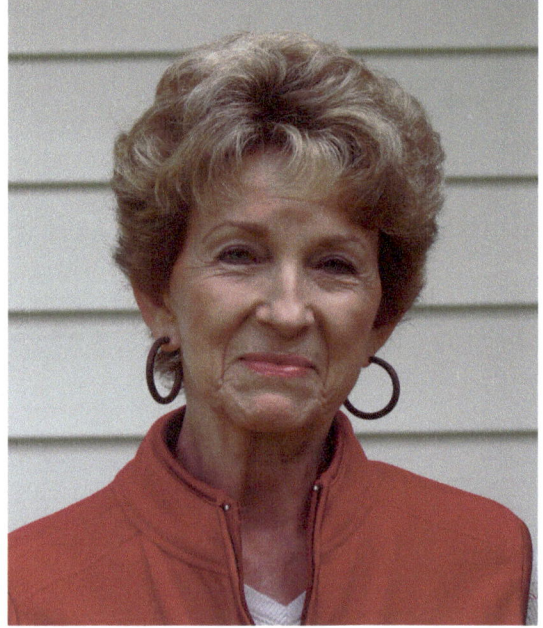

Tri

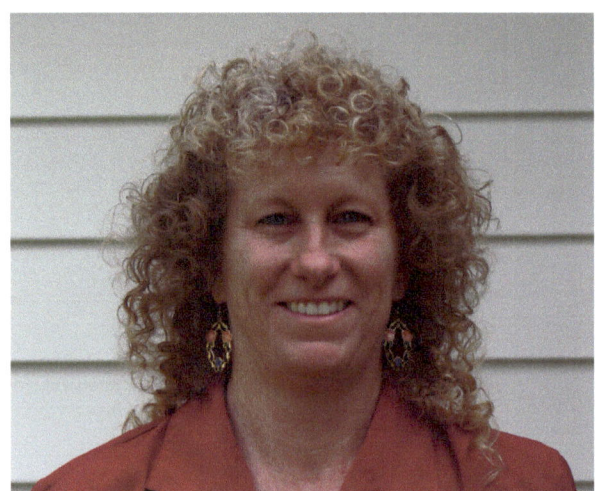

Nan

MeeMa

About the Author

Barbara Haney lives in eastern Washington state. She is fortunate to have one of her daughters living next door whose grand daughters come over to "hang out". Barbara has a desire for children to know God and the blessings He has for them. This book was conceived from this desire. You, too will be blessed as you share this book with your children.

www.ingramcontent.com/pod-product-compliance
Lightning Source LLC
Chambersburg PA
CBHW041307180526
45172CB00003B/1002